# Animal Coloring Book Cats: 50 Cool Cat Coloring Pages For Adults' Relaxation

## Coloring For Relaxation, Stress Relief, Inspiration, Mindfulness and Meditation

### Zen Edition

Relaxing Mandalas Volume 5

Dieses Malbuch gehört:_____

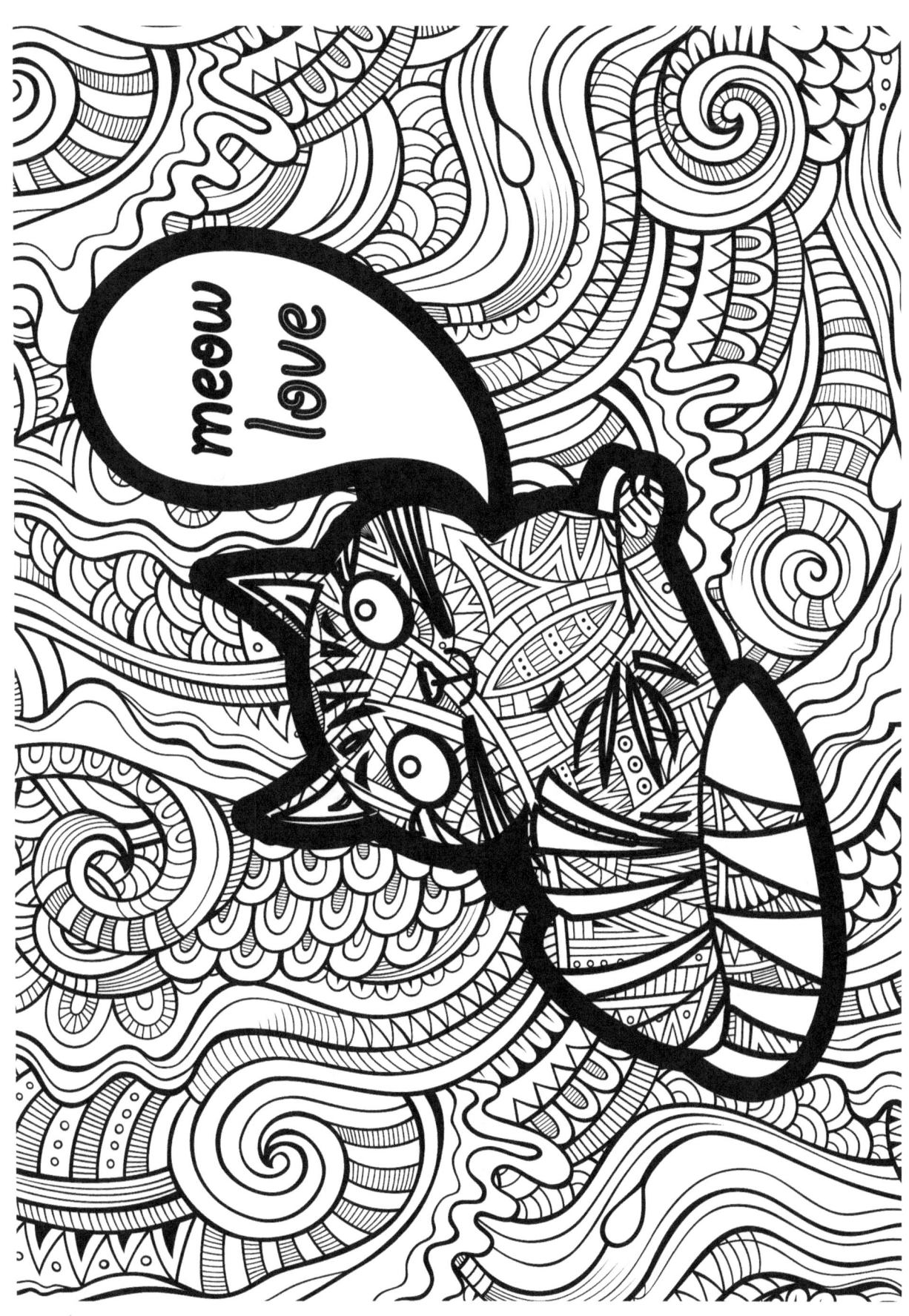

# More Great Coloring Books For You

 Paisley Adult Coloring Book Paisley Designs Coloring: Coloring for Inspiration, Meditation and Relaxation

 Animal Mandala Coloring Book: Relaxing Animal Mandala Coloring Pages: Coloring for Relaxation, Stress Relief and Meditation

 Mandala Coloring Book For Adults: 50 Easy Mandala Coloring Pages For Adults' Relaxation, Stress Relief and Meditation

 Mandala Coloring Book for Kids: 50 Mandala Coloring Pages: Coloring For Kids

Animal Mandalas Coloring Book for Adults: Butterflies and Flowers 80 Coloring Pages for Advanced Colorists

# You Might Also Enjoy These Activity Books

The Plant Based Diet Food Journal: Food Journal Diary for Women

My Favorite Recipes: Blank Cookbook

Fasting for Health Journal
Track Your Progress
Reap Your Fast Gains

Puzzle Challenge: Beginner's Crossword Puzzle Book

Horse Themed Weekly Journal: Event
Journal for Horse Lovers